Victims Of The System

The dark side of child welfare

by

James Hubbard

ISBN-13: (hardcover)
ISBN-13: (paperback)
ISBN-13: (ebook)
ISBN-13: (audiobook)

Although the author and publisher have made every effort to ensure that the information in this book was correct at press time, the author and publisher do not assume and hereby disclaim any liability to any party for any loss, damage, or disruption caused by errors or omissions, whether such errors or omissions result from negligence, accident, or any other cause.

This publication is designed to provide accurate and authoritative information with regard to the subject matter covered. It is sold with the understanding that the publisher is not engaged in rendering professional services. If legal advice or other expert assistance is required, the services of a competent professional should be sought.

The fact that an organization or website is referred to in this work as a citation and/or a potential source of further information does not mean that the author or the publisher endorses the information the organization or website may provide or recommendations it may make.

Introduction: Voices Silenced

Within the folds of society's most noble intentions often lie dark crevices where corruption festers, casting long shadows over the vulnerable. Nowhere is this division more pronounced than in the realm of child welfare—a system designed to be a sanctuary for the endangered but which has, in alarming cases, morphed into an arena of silent battles and suppressed cries.

In tracing the outlines of this system, we will not be wandering through the chambers of statistics and policy alone; we endeavor to hear the echoes of the lives that resonate within. This introduction lays the foundation for an inquiry into a child welfare system plagued not just by inefficiency but by something more insidious—a corruption that weaves through its very fabric, muting the voices of those it was intended to safeguard.

The stories are heartrending—a racket of truths muffled under the heavy blanket of institutional processes. And while the individuals caught in this web are diverse in their experiences and suffering, they share a common plight: the struggle to make their reality heard and understood. It's a narrative familiar to many victims of systemic failures: the cruel irony of a protectiveness that corrodes rather than shelters, of interventions that harm rather than heal.

One can't help but question: How did a system with such pure intentions become a source of pain?

Across the chapters that follow, the veil is slowly lifted, exposing the elements that contribute to this tragic paradox. Yet, we must recognize that to cast light on shadowy practices is only the beginning. Awareness, while vital, is not the terminus—it's the spark that ignites the long journey toward transformation.

Each chapter in this narrative takes us deeper into the warren, beyond the surface-level facade of protection and into the mechanisms that drive the child welfare system to fracture the very families it aims to keep whole. From legal battles that often feel like a setup for failure, to the foster care system's broken promises, the ensuing chapters unpack layers of malpractice and misguided policies.

But to understand the present, one must acknowledge the silenced speeches of the past—the whistleblowers and reformers who, despite the exorbitant personal cost, have raised alarms about the systemic rot within. Their stories, steeped in moral dilemmas and personal sacrifices, form an essential thread in the narrative fabric of this investigation.

In the face of adversity and against a backdrop of bureaucratic fortresses, there exists the resilient spirit of the human condition. It is a testament to those who refuse to be irreparably broken by a corrupted system. As we delve into the psychological scars and the quest for reform, we are reminded of the indomitable will to seek restoration and empowerment, not just for the individual, but for communities and society at large.

It is with a sobering clarity and a deep-felt urgency that this book asks you to listen—to not just the words on these pages, but to the resonances of the countless unheard stories they represent. This invitation to witness is extended with the hope that from understanding can emerge action, and from action, a reclaiming of hope and dignity.

The chapters to follow are not mere critique or grief; they are a call to recognize the flaws in our protective systems and to commit to the difficult task of mending them. Through introspective and informed discussion, it is possible to move towards a child welfare system that truly honors the rights and well-being of children and their families. The silenced voices do not have to remain silent forever; there is a chance yet for their stories to be heard and for their experiences to reshape a new legacy of care and justice.

Chapter 1: Unveiling the Facade of Protection

As we transcend the introductory echoes of silenced voices, it's essential to tear away the veil that obscures the true nature of what's benevolently called protection. This system, cloaked in the guise of aid and benevolence, frequently withers under the scrutiny of the discerning eye. We may begin our exploration by acknowledging a disheartening truth—the helping hand extended by the child welfare system can sometimes mask a firm grip that pulls at the very fabric of family unity.

The first tendrils of doubt creep in with the realization that assistance is not without its conditions and often comes in a form that deviates from the expected nurturing touch. ‘Protection’ has too often been a codeword for intervention that fails to discern the difference between the need for support and the impulse to segregate. It is within the subtleties of 'help' that families find themselves entangled, as systems designed to safeguard become the architects of division. The premise of safeguarding children is undisputedly noble, yet the execution can be marred by a maze of policy and practice that loses sight of individual humanity amidst a sea of cases and statistics.

As families navigate these disorderly waters, they encounter a paradox: the proclaimed sanctuary of the system weighs heavily against the anchors of familial bonds. Children become entwined in a net of procedures and protocols that are detached from the idiosyncratic needs of each human soul caught within. This chapter serves not as a blanket condemnation but as an eye-opener to the incongruities and challenges that must be addressed—a shrill call to lift the facade and confront the reality beneath the surface of protection.

The Disguise of Assistance

In the quest to understand the complexities of the child welfare system, we come upon a chameleon—the disguise of assistance. Through the promise of supporting vulnerable families and protecting children in perilous situations, what should be a service of compassion and support often metamorphoses into a mechanism of control that undermines the very essence of family unity and individual autonomy.

Every parent or guardian instinctively yearns to provide for their children's needs and to shield them from harm. Yet, when families find themselves under the scrutiny of child welfare services, that innate responsibility can be questioned, even usurped, under the banner of 'assistance.' Under this pretext, interventions are made—the kind of interventions that, rather than delivering the promised aid, frequently inflict inadvertent harm. Support systems are indeed crucial; there is no question to their potential to lift and aid. Yet, if they are not administered with a painstaking adherence to integrity and transparency, they can cloak hidden motives and result in a tapestry of unintended and sometimes devastating consequences.

Consider the scenario where assistance comes with strings attached—mandates that subtly coerce families to comply with certain interventions or risk being separated from their children. It's in this gray area where good intentions are cloaked with a bureaucratic veil, that families can unwittingly enter a vortex of control. Here lies the division of the welfare system: a reputed benevolent entity capable of wielding disconcerting power over those it is meant to serve.

The function of child welfare services should be clear-cut: to provide temporary, necessary support and return children to a safe and loving home environment as quickly as possible. However, within the cyclical nature of this system, families often feel lost, unsupported by a narrative that speaks of assistance but walks a path of punitive measures and invasive oversight.

Thus, this critique isn't so much about the individuals who serve within the system—many of whom embarked on this career out of a sincere desire to make a difference—but rather about the structural rigidity and policy frameworks that push the institution of child welfare into a role that parents didn't ask for and children don't always need. It is one thing to offer a lifeline; it's entirely another when that lifeline becomes a binding coil that families struggle to free themselves from.

To examine the disguise of assistance is to understand that when the system prioritizes its own preservation over the individual and familial autonomy it portends to uphold, it acts out of alignment with its stated purpose. In the forthcoming chapters, the focus shifts to disentangling monetary motives, legal quagmires, and ultimately, the corrosive impact on the psyche and overall well-being of those who endure these systemically flawed interventions.

```
```

Breaking Families Apart

The fundamental principle of any child welfare system is to shield the vulnerable youth from harm, ensuring their wellbeing is at the forefront of interventions. Yet, paradoxically, the same institutions erected to protect often precipitate a haunting reality: the fragmentation of families. The machinery of child welfare, for some, has become synonymous with the intrusion into family sanctuaries, dislodging the foundational stones of trust and unity for reasons that sometimes stray far from the welfare of the child.

Envision a household, teetering on the edge of stability due to socioeconomic strain or behavioral health challenges. Here, the system's intervention might indeed be justified at a glance. However, the criteria for such actions are seemingly fluid, and with troubling frequency, children are stolen from homes not on the grounds of imminent danger but as a default reaction to complexity. Yet, once a family is ensnared in the system's purview, the avenues to prove their capability and regain unity are often complex and fraught with bias.

Through this section, we delve into the narratives of families upended, examining the role of case workers and policy that apply a one-size-fits-all approach to diverse family dynamics. The bureaucracy, by its nature impersonal, lays the groundwork for a system where children are shuffled into foster care, sometimes unnecessarily. As we dissect this issue, stories emerge of parents whose infractions are minor—perhaps, a momentary lapse in judgment or a struggle with poverty that could be surmounted with community support rather than family separation.

The accounts are neither isolated nor uncommon. They represent a pattern, a systemic snare that contends with parental bonds through a prism of skepticism. Loss of custody often initiates a battle with an obscured endpoint. Parents confront a goliath in an arena where the presumption of innocence is inverted, and reunification is a gauntlet replete with judgements from those who haven't walked in their shoes. The emotional and psychological toll on children severed from their families resounds through their formative years, often carrying the echo of loss and confusion far into adulthood.

It's important to remember that each statistic is a heartbeat, every case file a living tapestry of hopes, dreams, fears, and affections. Within these pages, we acknowledge the deep scars incurred when a family is pulled apart, and the tremors felt across communities. It's a critical inquiry into whether this upheaval truly serves the best interests of the child or whether it's a reflection of a system that has forsaken the holiness of the family unit for protocol and procedure.

As we cross this touching topic, bear in mind the intent: not to undermine the genuine cases where separation is the only recourse for a child's safety, but to shed light on the instances where the system's compass seems to have gone crooked. Reflection is of greatest importance—the system tasked with safeguarding children must be scrutinized when it becomes the very storm from which families seek shelter.

Chapter 2: A System of Incentives and Penalties

In our exploration of the child welfare system's complications, we come upon a most perplexing and distressing realization—the presence of incentives and penalties that do not necessarily align with the welfare of children and families. Rather, they are artifacts of a system whose compass, at times, seems to steer by financial and statistical stars instead of by the welfare of its charges.

Consider the entities tasked with the protection and care of our most vulnerable—children under the custody of the state. These entities are rewarded for performance. But what metrics denote successful performance? Are they the metrics of family reunification, of the minimization of trauma, of the maximal growth and flourishing of children? If only that were the sure case. Instead, what we often find are incentives tied to financial consideration, to rates of adoption over reunification, to numbers that tell lack of appreciation of individual human experiences.

The currency of these incentives, however, is not strictly monetary. Professionals within the system may face implicit penalties—career stagnation, professional marginalization—should they defy the prevailing winds of policy or call into question the ethic of efficacy dictated by numbers and balance sheets.

One need not delve deep to witness the presence of these incentives. Foster care quotas, adoption targets, and federal funding lines speak of a landscape where the child is abstracted to a unit—a case number around which dollars flow. But a child is not a mere unit; a family is not simply a case. These are living, breathing realities, intricate tapestries of experience and emotion, generationally intertwined and in need of understanding beyond the cold calculus of systematized reward and penalty.

It is upon the shoulders of this system that a child's world may rest—a heavy and insecure burden. A well-intentioned move toward ensuring that no child is left without care has, in part, transmuted into a machine with its gears greased by fiscal policy, feeding into and being fed by a bustling foster care industry where the commodity is human potential.

In the pages following this one, we shall dissect these monetary motives, sparing no detail on how financial incentives have come to mold the contours of our child welfare practices. We will shed light on the quotas that quietly insinuate themselves into the lives of families, coercing a narrative of success that is not defined by smiles on children's faces but rather by completed forms and closed cases.

Monetary Motives in Child Welfare

There exists a disquieting motivation within the child welfare system, one that casts a long shadow over selfless intentions. Beneath the veneer of child protection and family support, financial incentives can implicitly shape policies and practices. It's a troubling notion to entertain: that the very institution entrusted with the safeguarding of our youth might, at times, be swayed by monetary gain over the best interests of the children it serves.

Consider, for instance, the funding mechanisms that drive the system. Federal contributions to state child welfare services are often allocated based on specific criteria and outcomes, which, paradoxically, can inadvertently encourage a numbers-driven approach to child intervention and foster care placements. It's an intricate dance of fiscal policy and social work, where the tempo is set by the ringing of cash registers rather than the measured pace of thoughtful care.

The perverse financial incentives do not exist in isolation; they are woven into the daily operations of child protective services. Budgets may swell with the increase in the number of children taken into custody, inadvertently setting a quota system that favors separation over family rehabilitation. The hum of bureaucracy harmonizes with the dissonance of children's lives being orchestrated by fiscal notes rather than their individual psychosocial needs.

There is an undeniable tension between the economics of child welfare and the ethics that should underpin it. While funds are indeed necessary for the operation of a robust child protective system, the question looms large: at what point does the influence of money begin to corrupt the purity of purpose? The dilemma isn't merely philosophical; it translates into real decisions that can fracture families and alter the course of young lives.

In dissecting the monetary motives in child welfare, we unravel the intricate tapestry of care and commerce. We expose the blemished narrative that often reads more like a ledger than a case file. Indeed, the fiscal underpinnings of child welfare agencies must be scrutinized and aligned with the irrefutable mandate to serve the best interests of children and their families. Otherwise, we run the risk of market forces dictating matters of the heart , which ought to be sacred and impervious to such influences.

Unraveling this narrative is crucial in advancing towards a system where money serves as a tool for empowering and healing, not as an invisible factor in decisions that may haunt children through their lifetime. We must reflect upon how to steer this vessel, heavy with the treasure of our future, back to its intended course—one charted by compassion and guided by justice.

The Cost of Quotas on Family Unity

The gears of bureaucracy grind in a constant march, often cold and indifferent. Within the child welfare system, quotas—benchmarks for how many children must be placed into foster care—exert an invisible pressure on social workers, transforming a mandate to protect into a relentless pursuit of numbers over nuanced need. It is not mere conjecture to suggest that these quotas can, and often do, rip families apart when a child is removed based on system demands rather than absolute necessity.

The irony is bitter; a system meant to safeguard becomes the saboteur, its web of incentives ensnaring those it intends to liberate. To meet these quotas, families are dissected at the surface without adequately exploring the potential for reunification or support. Children become pawns on a statistical chessboard, their placements shuffled to meet the demands of a ledger. This practice undermines the foundational principle of family preservation, meant to take precedence in the child welfare narrative.

A poignant truth looms: each number reached in meeting quotas marks a fracture in a family's story, a forced fissure in the heart of kinship. A single act of separation initiates a devastating event, each with a profound cost weighed in the currency of emotional bonds and shattered trust. When children are removed from their homes without careful contemplation or substantial evidence of harm, the very fabric of the family unit is at risk of irreparable damage.

Detachment from familiar surroundings, bonds of affection, and parental guidance—all these intrinsic elements of family that children rely on for their sense of security and identity—become collateral in the exchange to appease the quota. A home fractured by such mandates struggles to witness the rebirth of its once harmonious rhythm; reunification becomes difficult when trust in the system is eclipsed by the darkness of displacement.

Whether from the vantage of immediate pain or the long lens of perpetual consequences, the cost of quotas is steep. Emotional upheaval for children often manifests in behavioral issues, developmental delays, and psychological disorders. The repercussions are not isolated—they echo into society at large, a reverberation of a flawed system's dissonance. Can we then conclude that these quotas serve the interests of the vulnerable? Or do they reveal a system more concerned with self-preservation and the appearance of efficiency?

Critics of the system argue that a paradigm shift is among us . The mandate must center on the welfare of the family unit, seen not as an assembly of individuals susceptible to division, but as an integral whole. It is not just an operational change that is requisite; it is a restoration of values, a rekindling of empathy. We look toward a future where the unity of the family prevails over the shadowy mechanics of quotas, restoring hope where it has been withdrawn.

```
```

Chapter 3: Legal Battles Against Invisible Chains

Within the halls of justice, one may expect to find truth and fairness reigning supreme. However, it's imperative to understand that the law itself, as much as it aspires to be trustworthy, is often subject to the influence and manipulation of individuals who may not have pure intentions. Regrettably, when such manipulations occur within the child welfare system, it is the very fabric of family that is torn.

Families find themselves thrust into a complication of legal proceedings, overwhelmed by statutes and mandates they scarcely comprehend. The law, intended to act as a shield for the vulnerable, can paradoxically become a tool to ensnare them further—binding them with invisible chains that are as restrictive as they are intangible.

Consider the scenario where what's deemed 'best for the child' becomes a weapon rather than a safeguard. Legal professionals and caseworkers may be driven by various agendas—sometimes informed by policy, sometimes by profit. It becomes evident that the gulf between juvenile justice and injustice can hinge on the biases and objectives of those in control of the legal switchboard.

The struggles faced in the courtrooms aren't merely battles of expression or legal acuity; they are often a Crusade for the reclamation of one's voice against a system that can seem deaf to pleas of reason and compassion. Parents and guardians stride the tightrope of proving their competency and love for their children against an accusation-hungry opposition.

One can't help but inquire—where does protection end and prevarication begin? Should families be subjected to the whims and fancies of systems that speak of welfare but act as a mediator of division? The intersection between policy and humanity, between system and sensitivity, is fraught with tension and in need of meticulous scrutiny.

This chapter won't delve into the specifics of the manipulative tactics or the justice system's failings—that depth is reserved for the subsections to follow. Rather, this is an invitation to consider the daunting journey faced by scores of families. Each legal proceeding carries the weight of a child's future yet is often treated as just another file on a bureaucrat's desk.

We must ask ourselves, can the scales of justice truly balance the rights of the vulnerable against the might of the institution? As you navigate through the intricacies of what defines 'legal' in the child welfare system, the view widens to comprehend a landscape wherein the letter of the law is not always aligned with the spirit of justice. And so, the invisible chains are rendered visible—exposed for scrutiny, for debate, and ultimately, for rectification.

Manipulating the Law for Custody

The underpinnings of our child welfare system, intended to serve as the last defense for children's safety, too often yield to the manipulations of those who understand the intricate dance of the law. Within this sphere, the truth becomes flexible, and genuine concern for child welfare is sometimes overshadowed by the strategic play for custody – a game where the child's voice is subdued beneath the clamor of adult agendas.

Tactics to bend the legal framework to one's own advantage in custody disputes are countless. Deliberate delays are crafted, embedding parents and children in an exhaustive limbo. False allegations emerge from the shadows, casting unwarranted doubts on a parent's capability. Evidence is curated with an artful bias, painting misleading portraits to influence the judiciary's decisions. These maneuvers are not mere stories but are reflective of patterns that persistently erode the principles of justice.

Consider the balance scale of justice, its equilibrium so delicate, swayed not by truth's weight but by the force of manipulation – an environment ripe for those with foresight and resources. The law, an elaborate construct, becomes a tool not for unearthing the truth, but for those adept at navigation to exploit its corridors to veer outcomes towards their favored destination.

Furthermore, law enforcement and social workers, intended to be impartial advocates, can fall prey to their own biases, inadvertently becoming accomplices in the distortion of justice. A parent's social standing, eloquence, or even the attorney's prowess can tip the scales. As such, the cold halls of courtrooms can be unkind to those who lack the means or the sophistication to articulate their narratives within the confined language of the law. The most potent argument or the most heart-wrenching plea can be disemboweled by legal technicalities, losing their essence before reaching the ears for whom they're meant.

It's tragic, isn't it? The child, for whom the entire system supposedly operates, becomes a mere token in this complex game of chess. Each move, calculated; each play, laden with an intention that diverges from the child's interest. The law's spirit, manipulated by this crafty exploitation, gives rise to outcomes that may satisfy legal criteria but fail the essence of humanity and the heart of childhood's needs.

What then becomes of justice? What of the righteous path that should illuminate our society's moral compass? The path is there, but blinded by practices and tactics that serve not the vulnerable, the voiceless, but the strategically redundant. Witnessing this reflection, we must ask ourselves where the line is drawn between skillful advocacy and outright manipulation, and how the child's welfare can be safeguarded in the battlefields of custody wars.

```
```

Juvenile Justice or Injustice?

When traversing the complex pathways of the child welfare system, one can't help but confront a glaring paradox: the difference between juvenile justice and what feels like an overarching injustice. If we peer behind the veneer of legal proceedings designed to rehabilitate and protect, we often discover that these institutions are fraught with incongruences which undermine the very essence of justice that they should embrace. Our journey here is an exploration of this dissonance and a quest for deeper understanding.

In theory, juvenile courts are intended as a defensive wall, standing between youth and the potential punitive excesses of the adult legal system. They are meant to provide a second chance for children and adolescents whose lives have been marred by circumstances often beyond their control. However, in practice, these courts can become just another cog in a juddering machine, operating under the guise of rehabilitation, while systematically failing to address the roots of delinquency and neglect.

Consider the case of young individuals thrust into care for relatively minor infractions, often the fruits of socioeconomic inequality or systemic biases. Here, you might find a mire of overcrowded facilities where the invisible tentacles of psychological distress and social disadvantage entangle youth, leaving them more hardened than healed. Furthermore, the placement rates speak volumes: too many of these young souls return to care, indicating a cycle not broken, but rather perpetuated by the system purported to save them.

What then can we say of justice, if these children are trapped by invisible chains of a supposedly good system? It can't be ignored that the scales of justice are not evenly balanced; they tip heavily towards those with privilege—of means, of social standing, of support systems. For the disenfranchised, these scales represent not fairness, but a chronic tilt that favors their fall.

The truth is that harsh real-world consequences await these children. Opportunities for education, employment, and stable relationships are often irreparably damaged, leaving deep rifts that cannot be bridged by superficial interventions. While it's true that some may emerge from this system unscathed, the magnetic pull of its inflicting nature too often dominates, snatching the potential for transformative justice right from their grasp.

In unveiling these truths, we perceive a pattern of punitive measures misaligned with proactive, supportive care. This revelation is painful—yet necessary—to confront. It begs us to question, to challenge, and ultimately to dismantle these paradigms that do not serve the well-being or the future of the children caught in their snare. By highlighting this gross disparity between intent and outcome, we edge closer to the reformative action that is imperative for a system that doesn't just judge, but one that truly seeks justice for our youth.

Chapter 4: Foster Care Fallacies

In the midst of handling the complexities of child welfare, a narrative surfaces promoting the foster care system as a safe haven, a stabilizing solution for youths in turmoil. Yet, this chapter aims to dismantle such misconceptions by shedding light on the often grim reality of impermanence and disarray that shadows the lives of many foster children. As the tales of foster experiences unfold, we come to realize that the intended sanctuaries for these vulnerable individuals are, at times, no more than an illusion. In the strange cocktail of mismanagement and oversight, these young lives are tossed about on a turbulent sea, their anchors of hope and security seemingly slip away by the very system designed to protect them.

With each move from home to home, promise to promise, foster children collect fragments of a life that should have been whole. The statistics are staggering, yet beneath them lies an underbelly of lived experiences, of childhoods compressed into files and reports. The concept of a temporary shelter until a return to normalcy is frequently a misjudged calculation. Far too often, these temporary solutions calcify into purgatorial stretches that leave children in a stumble of developmental limbo, neither here nor there, ghosts in the vast machinery of child welfare. It's a challenging predicament, for as they grapple with their own emergent identities, foster children are also faced with conflicting needs for autonomy and belonging.

Moreover, the business of foster homes, couched in the language of care and compassion, conceals a telltale heartbeat of commerce. Within this financial framework, children become inadvertent commodities, and their best interests risk being wedged against fiscal policies and bottom lines. As this chapter delves deeper into the paradoxes of the foster care system, it becomes increasingly clear that the fallacies are not merely administrative errors but systemic flaws—flaws that require not just patches but profound transformation. This system, which holds the futures of countless children within its grasp, must be held accountable to the young souls it serves and endeavors to care for.

Impermanence and Instability: Foster Care's Broken Promises

Imagine a system that vows to be the sanctuary for the vulnerable but, instead, becomes a maze of impermanent placements, broken bonds, and unfulfilled promises. This is the troubled reality faced by many within the foster care system—a landscape where the ideal of stability is all but an illusion

The concept of foster care is steeply rooted in the moral conviction to protect and provide for children who have been displaced from their families. It is a contract of care, assuring a temporary yet secure haven until a child can either return home or find permanence through adoption. Yet, the lived experiences of numerous children tell a different narrative—one marked by inconsistency and disruption.

Instability is, regrettably, an inherent characteristic of the system. As one digs deeper, they discover a pattern of frequent moves between different homes and schools, each transition eroding the foundation that children require to thrive. These aren't merely statistics; they're profound disruptions that shape the trajectories of these young lives.

A young child, once removed from their family for reasons ranging from neglect to systemic failures, often finds themselves shuffled from one foster placement to another. Each move can signify a new beginning deprived of continuity or predictability. Bonds are built and, just as swiftly, torn apart. The promise of stability becomes an elusive dream—as tenuous as grains of sand slipping through desperate fingers.

Sadly, the consequences are neither short lived nor insignificant. The psychological ramifications are far-reaching. Children, in their formative years particularly, require a sense of permanence to develop a secure psychological and emotional foundation. The foster care system's revolving door not only breaks the promise of a stable home but inadvertently contributes to a sense of worthlessness and rejection.

Moreover, the variability in the quality of care provided by foster homes compounds the instability. Not all foster homes provide the same level of care, and some, horrifyingly, cloak mistreatment and neglect. The vow to protect becomes a broken echo when children find themselves in environments worse off than the ones they were removed from.

The reassurances of a better future ring hollow when the system structured to deliver such outcomes is marred by inconstancy and impermanence. It becomes evident that there's a division between the promises set out in the principles of foster care and the harsh day-to-day realities of those navigating through its turbulent waters.

As we bear witness to this cycle of instability, it demands a collective reckoning. The broken promises of foster care reflect a system in need of deep introspection and decisive action. It signals for an unflinching examination of not why the idealistic facade exists, but how it can be dismantled in favor of a system that truly delivers the stability and permanence it professes to provide.

In asserting this, we must remember that every child carries the inherent right to a secure and loving home. This is not merely an aspiration but a crucial foundation for their entire life trajectory. Restoration of these broken promises is more than an overhaul of a system; it's a restoration of hope, of dignity, of the very fabric of what it means to nurture our future generations. As stewards of that future, the responsibility weighs heavily on our collective conscience to demand and effectuate lasting change.

From Care to Commerce: The Business of Foster Homes

Previously, we have deconstructed the facade of foster care as mere custody and protection. Now, let us draw attention to how a system, designed to function as a haven for the dispossessed, has made a perverse shift into the realm of commerce. In an arena where the welfare of children should be paramount, it increasingly resembles a market, where young lives are commodified, and their predicaments are exploited for monetary gain.

In the complex interplay of child welfare, private companies and non-profit organizations are contracted to manage foster care placements. seemingly, this is to ensure better outcomes for children. Ideally, these organizations would be stalwarts of altruistic care, guardians against the ills of abandonment and neglect. And yet, amid the tapestry of stories and experiences, a disturbing pattern emerges where profit margins overshadow the tender task of nurturing young souls.

It's an open secret that financial incentives can distort the missions of these entities. For every child placed into a foster home, a stream of funding ensues from local and federal sources. The child becomes, through no fault of their own, not just a ward of the state but also the unit of a transaction. The longer the child remains within the system, the more sustained the financial contributions to the agency or foster home. The incentive thus aligns not with the swift reunification of the child with kin or the expeditious placement into a permanent loving home but rather with prolonging their stay within the system. This creates an unintended consequence of potentially converting the child welfare system into a business that has supply and demand dynamics at play rather than a refuge for vulnerable youths.

Moreover, unreliable evidence and research hint at the unsettling possibilities of foster homes being prioritized over reunification with biological families. The longer a child remains in foster care, the more entrenched the financial streams become for the managing entities. The scale and reach of this issue are not uniform, varying from region to region, agency to agency. However, the very existence of such a misalignment begs the question - where is the malfunction that prioritizes the welfare of the child over the financial welfare of the system?

This commodification of foster children also manifests in excessive adversarial legal tactics employed to retain children in foster care. The cost is twofold: the emotional toll on children and families, and the financial burden on the taxpayer. Within this paradigm, it can be alarmingly easy for the child to feel like a pawn in a larger game, a game where the rules are rigged and the objectives skewed towards the financial vitality of the foster care business, rather than the flesh and innocents of the child’s life.

As we unveil this uncomfortable reality, it's incumbent upon us to ask ourselves – have we collectively hesitated? How have we allowed a system, believed to be one of the most respected support structures in society, to drift into this murky terrain of commerce? Critical examination of this paradigm is not only a duty but a necessary step towards reformation—where the child, not the dollar, is placed at the center of every decision, every policy, every home that bears the name foster.

Chapter 5: Psychological Scars and Permanent Damage

Continuing from our exploration into the underbelly of the child welfare system, we pivot our gaze to the indelible marks it leaves upon its young victims. The landscape of a childhood disrupted by systematic failures is riddled with deep grooves of psychological imprints that often evolve into lifelong struggles. Despite the outward facade that systems have your best interests at heart, we must critically examine the residual impact on those it has stirred up through its cogs.

Childhood Trauma: The Invisible Wounds

The impacts of separation from family, coupled with the torments of an overburdened foster care system, inflict wounds far beyond what the eyes can see. Childhood trauma isn't simply a fleeting storm, passing through a child's life and leaving behind a clear sky—it is more similar to a pervasive mist that saturates the very fabric of their being. Even as time marches forward, these invisible wounds often remain, shaping perceptions, reactions, and the nature of one's inner dialogue.

When a child's trust is compromised by the very institutions meant to protect them, we're not just failing them in the present. We're etching into their psyche a narrative that the world is inherently unsafe, that guardians can't be trusted, and that instability is the norm. These formative experiences, when left unaddressed, can harden into patterns of behavior that obscure the potential for healthy relationships and personal growth in adulthood.

Long-term Impacts of Flawed Interventions

If only the story ended at mere psychological difficulty. The tapestry of a life altered by the system's interventions showcases a complex interplay of psychological, social, and physical dimensions. It's not simply a question of childhood hardships—these experiences carry a risk of becoming a continuation in adult life. The intervention of a flawed system can lead a path towards academic struggles, difficulty in securing stable employment, and susceptibility to substance abuse.

The pervasiveness of these outcomes cannot be overstated. We must acknowledge how the persistence of trauma’s echoes encumbers one’s path to fulfillment and self-realization. When society's structures, designed to aid in development, become the obstacles themselves, it is not merely an individual tragedy; it's a societal one. Systemic breakdowns that contribute to the declining mental health of those who have aged out of the child welfare system are much more than personal failings—they are the permanent damages we've inscribed upon the next generation.

In sum, the divide between the child welfare system's intentions and its outcomes can no longer be ignored. As we forge ahead, we need to carry the weighted knowledge that our societal structures have not only fallen short but have actively contributed to the festering of psychological scars. It is necessarily upon us to bear witness to these truths and, in doing so, to strive relentlessly for a future where the system's failures are not written into the life stories of its supposed beneficiaries.

Childhood Trauma: The Invisible Wounds

Often go undetected by the watching world, yet they resonate through the corridors of a child's psyche, long after their inception. Within the complex painting of the child welfare system, the intent is seemingly to safeguard the vulnerable. However, all too often, the means by which this protection is executed not only disrupts the present but unforgettably taints the canvas of the future. The trauma inflicted is not always apparent to the naked eye, but its reverberations are deeply felt, manifested in a whisper, a shiver, or a shadow upon a child's life that darkens prospects and joy.

The system, designed as a shield, can transform into a gavel, not of justice, but of judgment and separation. In the pursuit of addressing familial issues, children are sometimes abruptly uprooted, severed from familiar anchors without ceremony or sensitivity. It's in these critical moments that invisible wounds are inflicted—emotional abrasions and scars that don't bleed visibly but excape internally. These wounds, shaped by fear, uncertainty, and isolation, become the silent companions of those who experience the bowels of a system that loses sight of individual humanity in the face of procedural necessity.

These emotional and psychological injuries may not show up on the body, yet they manifest through behaviors and emotional instability that society is quick to misjudge. A system that should be healing instead often exacerbates distress through the lack of continuity and security. For a child, the loss of a parent or caregiver, coupled with the uncertainty of foster placements, can etch deep lines of trust issues and attachment disorders into their developing psyche, impair their relationship blueprint. The child, unable to voice or even comprehend the source of their anguish, carries a burden that is often invisible to the caretakers substituting for their lost familial bonds.

Indeed, this injury lurking beneath the surface tends to resurface in various forms: struggles in academic environments, difficulty in forming meaningful relationships, and engagement in self-destructive behaviors. These are not merely phases or traits, they are echoes of pain, calls for help that many fail to interpret accurately. Though the certainty of these impacts may escape the very professionals sworn to uphold the welfare of these young souls, the truth remains that a system that inflicts such wounds cannot claim to act in the best interest of the child.

The trauma inflicted in the formative years by the very instruments designed to protect can distort a child's world view, transforming it into a landscape where adults are distrusted, systems are oppressive, and help is a synonym for hurt. Yet, recognition and acknowledgment are the first steps toward healing. One cannot mend what one refuses to believe is broken. As we delve deeper into the psychological scars and the permanent damage that the system can, unwittingly or otherwise, leave in its wake, it's vital to understand that the path ahead requires courage, not only to confront the flaws but to innovate with empathy and understanding.

Addressing these invisible wounds calls for a shift in perspective, moving from a paradigm of punitive enforcement to one of restoration and genuine nurturing.

It requires the entire community—professionals, caregivers, and society at large—to become attuned to the silent cries of childhood trauma. Only when the system is capable of seeing beyond the surface, of treating not just the symptom but the hidden ailment, can hope for recovery and restoration begin to take root. As we inch forward with resolve, let us not forget those carrying the invisible wounds, for it is in their healing that the true measure of our collective humanity will be found.

Long-term Impacts of Flawed Interventions

When we consider the intricate web that forms a child's developmental environment, any intervention — particularly a flawed one — can resonate across the span of their entire life. The tendrils of these actions are far-reaching, touching upon every surface, from psychological wellbeing to societal engagement. It's paramount to understand that when interventions in a child's life are mishandled, the repercussions are not merely immediate or fleeting; they can extend far into adulthood, shaping an individual's identity, relationships, and capacity to function in the world.

The idea of intervention, inherently, is a double-edged sword — poised to protect or to inflict unseen harm. In the realm of child welfare, interventions are substantiated with the solemn promise to safeguard the vulnerable. However, flawed interventions often emerge from a system fraught with issues; a system that sometimes prioritizes policy over people, and incentives over individual needs.

Flawed interventions can manifest in various forms. A premature or incorrect removal of a child from their home, or the failure to provide appropriate and nurturing foster care, both examples represent clear departures from the intent to protect and support. Bonds are torn apart, vital connections with family and community severed, often under the advocacy of safeguarding the child. But what looms in the aftermath?

Children uprooted from their homes and thrust into the foster care machinery frequently grapple with the loss of stability and identity. The familial tapestry that once narrated their existence is now a patchwork of temporary shelters and hollow promises. Such disruptions can lead to developmental delays, persistent feelings of abandonment, and difficulties in forming secure attachments later in life. The impact on mental health is profound; anxiety, depression, and behavioral disorders become the unwanted companions of many.

Academically, these children often fall behind, their education fractured by frequent relocations and emotional turmoil. This in turn molds their future prospects, as educational attainment is closely linked to economic stability and career opportunities. The system's failure to provide a consistent and conducive learning environment reverberates long after these children have transitioned into adulthood. The envisioned protection morphs into repression, as their potential is deprived by the very measures intended to uplift them.

In the social landscape, the repercussions are equally distinct. Having viewed the world through the unpredictable lens of the system, these individuals may struggle with trust and social integration. Relationships become battlegrounds where vulnerability is a liability, where reliance on another is tantamount to risking another abandonment. A deep-seated sense of isolation can settle within the soul, not so much a choice as a learned survival mechanism.

Economically, the impact is just as tangible. Fostered individuals often face an abrupt end to support systems as they reach the age of majority; a sharp cut-off that leaves little room for a gradual transition to independence. They are expected to function as self-sufficient adults, yet how can this be the expectation when the very scaffoldings of support were flawed or altogether missing during their formative years?

In criminality, the correlation is inhumane. Studies indicate a relatively large number of individuals in the juvenile and criminal justice systems have histories within foster care. It is not to suggest an inherent tendency for crime within these individuals but rather to spotlight the failure of interventions that instead of rehabilitating, inadvertently prime a path toward incarceration. The safety net becomes a funnel, guiding too many toward confinement instead of community contribution.

As we navigate the ongoing discourse on child welfare, it is critical to remain vigilant about the long-term impacts of flawed interventions. Only through the lens of holistic compassion and deep understanding can we begin to rectify the failings and weave a new narrative for the coming generations—one that truly honors the innocents and potential of each young life entrusted to the care of the system.

Chapter 6: Whistleblowers and the Truth They Reveal

In the center of the child welfare system, there exists a small group of individuals whose courage illuminates the dark recesses of bureaucracy and vested interests. These whistleblowers, often standing alone against a powerful organization, offer an uncloaked view into the convoluted realms where ideals of child protection lose their way, morphing into unrecognizable entities that serve purposes far from their original mandate.

The voices of these individuals are like lighthouses in a fog-dense sea, providing direly needed navigation points for charting a course toward integrity. When they bear witness to misdeeds, their testimonials can tear through the fabric of normality that clothes a dysfunctional system. The path of a whistleblower is fraught with risk, as the institutions they challenge often wield substantial power to quash them, embedding fear and silence as the main currency of their kingdom.

Consider the persistence it requires to not only recognize and internalize the wrongdoing but also to have the audacity to raise one's voice in a loud call for change. Blowing the whistle is never done lightly; it's propelled by a profound belief in rectitude and an understanding that truth—however inconvenient or disruptive—retains its value and demands its day.

In revealing what lies beneath the polished veneer of the child welfare system, these brave souls showcase the adverse effects of policies and actions that are rarely scrutinized with adequate vigor. Their stories are beacons that wave the attention of the public and policymakers alike, summoning a moral imperative to not only listen but to act.

Yet, laying bare such truths is not without cost. Retaliation is a stark reality for many who step into the light, yielding their personal tranquility as payment for the public's enlightenment. Harsh retaliations might take the form of professional cold shouldering, legal battles, and at times, personal threats.

Still, the moral victory that comes with bringing truth to the surface cannot be overshadowed by these offenses. Knowledge once kindled cannot be unburned—it carries the power to ignite systemic transformation and renewed accountability. As we explore the narratives of those who have dared to reveal the tangling vines of corruption and negligence, we should ponder the strength it would take to join their ranks, should we ever face such a calling. Through their experiences, we glean piercing insights into the need for fundamental reform and begin to map the terrain for a system that truly upholds the best interests of children and their families.

Let us heed the revelations brought forth by whistleblowers as more than mere tales of courage in the face of adversity. Let them serve as a testament to the boundless potential for transformation when truth becomes the cornerstone of collective action. These whistleblowers are not just voices from within the system—they are the vanguards of hope for a future where the child welfare system fulfills its noblest

purpose to nurture and protect, without compromise or corruption.
```
```

The Voices From Within the System

In the dimly lit corners of the child welfare system, far beyond the public eye, there is an undercurrent of urgency whispered by those who labor within its confines. These are the voices of social workers, case managers, and even judges - the very sinews and bones of a system purportedly designed to protect the most vulnerable. But as they navigate the mazelike corridors of policies and procedures, a dissonant chorus rises, highlighting inherent contradictions and disrupting the pervasive silence that cloaks systemic misconduct.

Occasionally, amidst the racket of silent suffering and institutional noise, a voice of clarity emerges. It might be a caseworker, burdened with an impossible caseload, who observes the dehumanizing tick boxes that reduce the rich tapestry of human life to sterile statistics. Or perhaps it's a guardian, who after witnessing one too many hollow victories in the courtroom, questions whether the legal battles truly prioritize the child's well-being, or merely serve as a front for deeper systemic issues.

The voices from within are not amplified by megaphones or broadcast on the nightly news; they are often muffled, hushed by veiled threats of professional repercussions or by the weight of a culture that suggests turning a blind eye is part of the job. Their stories, whispered in confidence to those who choose to listen, shed light on the incongruence between the noble mission statements etched on government walls and the grinding gears of a machine that sometimes seems to churn more harm than healing.

Consider the testimony of a seasoned social worker, whose career has been dedicated to reuniting families, yet who is constantly confronted with a system that seems more intent on tearing them apart for reasons that have more to do with policy than with compassion. Or the former foster youth turned advocate, speaking out against the cycle of displacement and emotional upheaval that has become an accepted norm within foster care, so radically at odds with the concept of nurturing guidance and stability.

These internal voices are a critical instrument for the health of the child welfare system. They offer invaluable insight into the day-to-day realities that are easily obscured by data reports and success metrics. Through their testament, we glimpse the heartrending choices they are forced to make under the compulsion of flawed directives. We see the dissonance between their professional obligations and personal convictions, between what is and what ought to be. It's essential that these voices are not just heard but taken into mind, for in them lies the potential for profound systemic transformation.

The courage to come forth and share these realities signifies more than personal bravery; it is an act of profound moral clarity. When the system itself seems tinged with corruption, the voices from within challenge us to confront uncomfortable truths and to seek solutions that align with the authentic purpose of safeguarding children and empowering families. They are the beacons guiding us toward a more compassionate, more just child welfare system. And if we're to move toward genuine reform, it's not only critical that we amplify these voices - we must integrate their insights into the very fabric of change.

Retaliation and the Cost of Truth

In the heart of a system cloaked under the guise of welfare lies the dangerous path of those who dare to expose its shadowed flaws. Whistleblowers, those brave souls who become the voice of the unheard, often find themselves facing a storm of retaliation. They embody the archetype of the solitary warrior, battling not against external foes, but against the very institution they sought to serve.

The cost of truth is often steep, and when it relates to the child welfare system, it spirals into a currency of personal sacrifices. Individuals reveal the unethical practices, who pinpoint the knots of corruption tightening around the cores of innocent families, are frequently met with the harsh backlash from those invested in the preservation of the status quo.

Retaliation is not a mythic entity from tales of ancient times; it is a visible, contemporary reality. It can manifest in career derailment, the formulating of professional isolation, and the unraveling of personal reputation. Employers may wield administrative actions as weapons, striking through demotion, unwarranted disciplinary measures, or outright termination. The psychological toll, the stress of anticipated backlash, parallels a form of warfare where the battleground is the whistleblower's every day life.

Yet, the amount of personal cost is not a tale of mere voluntary sufferers. It is a raw illustration of the bravery required to challenge the behemoths within bureaucratic mazes. Whistleblowers provide us a looking glass into the misdeeds sewn into the fabric of commendable institutions. They push us to question whether the scales of justice are truly balanced within the walls of child welfare agencies. Each story of retribution is a piece in the mosaic of truth, a truth that carries an unreasonable price for the individuals who summon the courage to speak it.

Moreover, the impact ricochets beyond the individual; it permeates the narrative of society's integrity. When the champions of truth face the threat of retaliation, it induces a chilling effect. A culture of silence is encouraged, where the fear of consequence cripples potential objectors, leaving systemic failures to fester unnoticed and unchallenged.

How, then, can these guardians of the vulnerable navigate this difficult journey? Legal protections exist, yet their shield is all too often penetrable. The road to justice and the restoration of one's integrity is dark, daunting, and arguably, a reflection of the hero's path—a journey of formidable challenges, loaded with trials of character and resilience.

Retaliation against whistleblowers is not merely an attack on individuals; it is an assault on the very concept of accountability. It is an attempt to mute the messengers of inconvenient truths, to stamp out the stirrings of reform. By acknowledging this, we confront the distressing implication that often in the world we inhabit, those who reveal uncomfortable truths bear unspeakable costs.

Within this sub-section, we have peeled back the layers to reveal the stark nakedness of whistleblowers' trials. We are reminded that to stand for truth is not a passive act but one brimming with potential sacrifice.

The path toward a reformed child welfare system is laden with obstacles, but recognizing situation of whistleblowers propels us to address the unjustified and foster a culture that not only protects, but respect those who lift the veil on hidden injustice.

Chapter 7: Toward Reform and Restoration

The path to healing and justice for victims of a system designed for protection yet steeped in corruption is difficult, but not impossible. As we transition from laying bare the deep-seated issues within the child welfare system, a loud call emerges—one that beckons us toward the vital work of reform and restoration. This chapter seeks to cultivate the ground toward meaningful change, recognizing the innate capacity within communities to foster resilience and advocate for the welfare of every child.

The pursuit of reform must be emboldened by the narratives of those who have suffered at the hands of malfunctioning institutions. The pain etched in their stories serves as a potent motive for the reconstruction of systems that have, for too long, operated under the guise of beneficence while perpetuating cycles of harm. Yet, it is not enough to be moved by these stories. Action must follow empathy, and strategies for change must be as dynamic and informed as the forces that oppose them. With pressing evidence of flaws and testimonies of those affected, comes the responsibility to rectify the wrongs and pave new avenues for protection and care that truly honor the dignity of the family unit.

In imagining a reformed child welfare landscape, we confront the necessity of holistic approaches—ones that address not only the symptoms but also the root causes. It is here that we find our blueprint for change: a comprehensive proposal for overhauling the system which must be anchored in the best interests of the child, supported by evidence-based practices, and upheld by a framework of accountability. This blueprint delineates the steps for a thorough re-evaluation of existing policies and practices, ensuring that every action is tailored to promote healing and prevent the needless severing of familial bonds. Building upon lessons learned, this new model demands continuous oversight, feedback, and public transparency to nurture an environment of trust where every voice is heard and valued.

Flowing from the wellspring of reform is the essential task of empowering families and communities. It is a mission that begins with trusting in the innate capacities present within familial structures and local networks. True empowerment means providing support without disempowerment, offering assistance without abduction. It means recognizing the strengths within communities—often marginalized or overlooked—and investing in those strengths to foster resilience and self-sufficiency. Strategies for empowerment will lean on local wisdom, enable access to resources, and provide education that equips families with the tools to thrive amidst adversity. By doing so, the child welfare system can transform from a punitive force into a partner for progress, nurturing the seeds of potential in every child and family.

In the face of a pressing need for reform and the daunting task of restoration, there stands an unwavering commitment to the principle that each child's well-being is intimately tied to the health of the family and the community. This chapter lays down the challenge before us—to re-imagine a system that truly serves the best interests of the child, while honoring the sacredness of the family. It is a call to march towards that day when trust is restored, communities are strengthened, and families can flourish without the shadow of unwarranted intervention. In this journey toward healing and justice, every step forward is an act of fierce compassion—a testament to the belief that while the work is rigorous, the cause is righteous and the outcomes, when achieved, will be reverently celebrated by all who cherish the promise of youth.

Blueprint for Change: Proposals for System Overhaul

In the quest to reimagine a child welfare system that genuinely serves the interests and well-being of children and their families, we must unfold the blueprints for transformative change. To erect new foundations where the old ones have cracked necessitates bold, courageous proposals that confront the systemic flaws we have unveiled.

Imagine a landscape where the primary measure of success within the child welfare system is the well-being of the child and the integrity of their family, rather than the sheer number of cases processed or the speed with which children are moved to foster care. We are at a crucial juncture where voices of dissent ring true and clear against the delusion of traditional operations.

The first pillar in our reconstruction is accountability. Our proposal demands the establishment of independent oversight bodies with the power to investigate, audit, and hold the child welfare system accountable for its actions. These bodies must possess the might to drive change, harnessing both the fury of injustice and the meticulousness of an auditor's inspection. We must weave transparency into the very fabric of the child welfare process, ensuring that every decision made can stand the test of public scrutiny and withstand the highest moral and ethical standards.

Reform requires not only the demolition of harmful practices but also the creation of nurturing, supportive alternatives. A revamped system would focus on preventative measures—providing families with the resources, education, and support they need to flourish without unwarranted government intervention. When removal is absolutely necessary, it should be coupled with a strong, clear path to reunification that prioritizes maintaining family connections and cultural heritage.

To empower these changes, we must overturn the current incentives that favor family separation. Financing models must be reformed to support family preservation and reunification, rather than funding foster care placements. We must invest in the very communities that have been stripped of their vitality, channeling funds into mental health services, addiction treatment, poverty reduction, and educational opportunities.

In the legal arena, our blueprint advocates for guaranteed legal representation for parents and children involved in the child welfare system. Just as one would not enter battle without a shield, no family should have to navigate these treacherous waters without an advocate by their side. It's not solely about legal prowess but the upholding of justice and the protection of the family unit.

In terms of placement, group homes and institutional settings should be the option of last resort, untied from financial gain, with foster care placements deliberately and mindfully chosen to emphasize stable, nurturing environments. The capacity of foster caregivers to provide quality, emotionally supportive care must be thoroughly evaluated, as the implications of mismatched placements are too severe to be gambled with.

The heart of our blueprint beats for prevention, early intervention, and the holistic treatment of families. It pulses with the conviction that when families are given the tools to succeed, they often do. Every branch of this proposed system from intervention agents to the judiciary, must embody a philosophy that sees the family as an ecosystem where each part supports the others—where support does not mean intrusion and where help does not equate to coercion.

This overhaul is not merely an exercise in policy change; it is a fundamental shift in the culture and the consciousness of the child welfare system. It is about erecting a new paradigm, grounded in respect, compassion, and the unshakeable belief that families are the cornerstone of society. It is a call to action for those who care for the future of our children and ultimately, the soul of our communities.

As we step into the fertile grounds of change, each proposal we put forth is a seed of hope. Together, by nurturing these seeds and diligently tending to the growth that follows, we embark on a journey of creating a system that does not just prevent harm but actively promotes healing and wholeness—a system worthy of the children and families it serves.

Empowering Families and Communities

Arises as a beacon of action, a call to arms that resonates in the depths of one's humanity. In the shadow of a system full of corruption and greed, the light of empowerment must emerge from the very fabric of those it aims to mend. This is the pulsing core of reform where the rebuilding begins. It's not a distant ideal but an immediate reality flowering from the seeds of collective engagement and support.

Empowerment is not the transient handover of resources, but the enduring act of strengthening familial bonds and catalyzing community resilience. The pathway here is dual; it entails fortifying the individual from the inside while simultaneously nourishing the community that envelops them. Within families, this means ensuring that parents and caregivers are afforded the education, tools, and support systems to navigate the maze that is child welfare—armoring them not with false promises but with the fierce guardianship of knowledge and rights.

Communities, when in good health, act as shield of social support, allowing the best outcomes for children to flourish. Empowered communities are havens wherein families are not isolated in their struggles but are part of an intricate network of care, where experiences and advice are shared threads in a larger supportive tapestry. Here lies the transformative power of community-based initiatives—programs that aren't blueprint duplicates but carefully crafted responses to the unique challenges and strengths of each locale.

The time-honored principle of 'it takes a village to raise a child' is not mere folklore but a creed to be woven into the fabric of societal reforms. Empowering local groups—a patchwork of nonprofits, faith-based organizations, and community leaders—enables a grassroots approach that's more alert and adaptive to the needs of its children and families than any monolithic system could ever be. These microcosmic societies stand as sentinels, both protective and healing, able to identify and address the challenges that families face in their daily lives.

Ultimately, empowerment demands a reckoning with the truths penned by those who dared to blow the whistle. It is in listening to and acting upon these revealed truths that systemic change ignites. When families and communities are empowered, the stranglehold of corruption loosens its grip, and we pave a road to a future where the child welfare system supports, rather than undermines, the holiness of family and the welfare of its youngest and most vulnerable members.

Conclusion: Reclaiming Hope and Dignity

In the wake of the revelations and narratives outlined in this volume, one could easily fall prey to hoplesness. Yet, when we delve into the depths of despair caused by the betrayal of the child welfare system, we must remember that it is within our grasp to rise again, to rebuild the shattered foundations of trust and care that should have been unfailing. Let us recognize that while the system has indeed failed many, it is within the capacity of every individual and community to enact real, tangible, and positive change.

The path to reclaiming hope and dignity lies not in the complete abandonment of our reformative intent, but in a radical shift in perspective. We must look beyond the conventional methods that have proven futile and instead find innovative ways to empower those who have been marginalized by the system. Our approach must be twofold—addressing both the systemic issues and healing the psychological scars left on innocent lives. Like the phoenix rising from the ashes, there is profound strength in reclaiming one's sense of self-value and place in the world after facing such adversity.

Hope is not just a fleeting emotion; it is a catalyst for action, a driving force that can lead us toward a more equitable and just society. It emboldens victims to become survivors, advocates, and reformers in their own right. Dignity, that fundamental human right, is retrieved through spirited perseverance, unwavering in our resolve to stand up against the inefficiencies and corruption that have long plagued the child welfare system.

All around us, there are individuals who have transcended their struggles and are now inspiring beacons for others who still grapple with the shadows of a painful past. Their lives are testaments to the power of resilience and the human spirit's capacity to overcome adversity. These stories don't just end with mere survival—they ascend to the creation of a context where individuals bear the torch of transformation, igniting the hope in others to bravely step forward and demand change.

To reclaim hope and dignity is a collective mission. It requires ongoing dialogue, ceaseless advocacy, and proactive involvement from all societal sections. The reform we seek must strike at the roots of systemic dysfunction and elevate the discourse to one that prioritizes preventative measures, family unity, and the genuine wellbeing of children. We need policies that are not merely words on the statute books, but living, breathing embodiments of justice and protection.

As we close the pages of this discourse, may we carry within us the unwavering belief that our efforts are not in vain. The journey toward healing and systemic rebuild is long, and there will be obstacles, but every step taken is a move closer to the world where every child and every family is treated with the reverence and respect they deserve. May each one of us be a vessel of hope and a harbinger of dignity, for in the grand tapestry of society's progress, every stitch counts. The time for change is now, and it begins with us.

```
```

Appendix A: Resources for Victims and Advocates

Navigating the child welfare system's rabbit hole can be an isolating journey, similar to traversing a complex maze with no visible exit. But even amidst the darkest corridors, flecks of light beckon—resources that can arm victims and advocates with the knowledge, support, and fortitude to challenge a seemingly indomitable adversary.

For those who've felt the strain of a system riddled with contradictions, the following resources are designed to serve as a beacon. They provide a starting point for empowerment and the groundwork for demanding accountability and pursuing justice.

Legal Aid and Representation

National Legal Aid & Defender Association (NLADA): Offers connections to legal aid and public defense for individuals in need.

Legal Services Corporation (LSC): Promotes equal access to justice in the U.S. by providing funding to legal aid organizations.

American Bar Association (ABA) Child Custody Pro Bono Directory: Connects individuals seeking child custody assistance with pro bono legal resources.

Counseling and Support Groups

Rainbow of Love Family Services: Offers emotional support and counseling to families navigating the child welfare system.

Parents Anonymous: A community of parents, organizations, and volunteers offering support and advocating for system reform.

Child Welfare Information Gateway: Provides information, resources, and tools covering child welfare, child abusc and neglect, foster care, and adoption.

Advocacy and Reform Organizations

Children's Rights: A national watchdog organization fighting to ensure the rights of children in foster care are respected and protected.

Child Welfare League of America (CWLA): Advocates for best practices in protecting and caring for children and youth.

Families Against Mandatory Minimums (FAMM): Works to reform the juvenile justice laws that impose mandatory sentences or treat minors as adults.

Support for Whistleblowers

Government Accountability Project (GAP): Provides protection and support to individuals who uncover wrongdoing within government agencies, including child welfare systems.

Whistleblower Support Fund: Offers assistance and advocacy for those who've bravely exposed corruption or dangers to public health and safety.

Educational Resources and Publications

The Child Welfare Trauma Training Toolkit: Offers training for professionals seeking to understand and mitigate the impact of trauma on children in the system.

Family Defense Handbook: Guides families on their rights and how to navigate legal challenges within the child welfare system.

Representing Parents in Child Welfare Cases: A manual for attorneys representing parents in child welfare cases that also sheds light on the legal processes involved for advocates and families.

Legally Kidnapped. By Carlos Morales.

The Constitutional Protector Against Cps. By Malibu Dallas

Fighting CPS, guilty until proven innocent of child protective services charge. By Deborah K. Frontiera

Within this reservoir of resources lie the tools for reclamation: legal support to challenge injustices, emotional support to weather the storms of custody battles, and educational materials which illuminate the complexities of the system. With tenacity, unity, and the wealth of assistance available, victims and advocates can press forward, transforming personal struggles into movements for reform—a march toward a future where families are fortified rather than fractured, where systems serve rather than conquer.

Made in the USA
Middletown, DE
23 December 2023

45310835R00040